On Skating

On Skating

By Gerhard Ulrich Anton Vieth

Translated by B. A. Thurber

Skating History Press

Main text originally published in German in 1789 and 1790.
Translation, introduction, and notes © 2022 B. A. Thurber.
All rights reserved.

ISBN: 978-1-948100-09-0
LCCN: 2022923417

Skating History Press
Evanston, IL
http://www.skatinghistorypress.com/

Contents

Introduction 1

Vieth in skating history 3

Vieth's life and work 9

Translator's note 17

On Skating 19

Foreword 21

Skating 25

Klopstock's poems 51
    Skating 51
    Braga 54
    Tialf's Art 57

Commentary 63

Notes 65

Further reading 75

Bibliography 77

Illustration credits 81

List of Figures

1	Portrait of G. U. A. Vieth.	10
2	Memorial for Vieth in Hooksiel.	14
3	Memorial for Vieth in Dessau.	15
4	Skating in a straight line.	41
5	Skating on a curve.	42
6	The spiral line created by a skater. . . .	47
7	A coin rolling on a curve	49
C1	A Breinermoor skate.	73

Introduction

Vieth in skating history

Gerhard Ulrich Anton Vieth's little book has gone down in history as the first book on skating published in German and the second in any language. It is a transcript of a lecture he gave in 1788 and first appeared, in article form, in 1789. The book version was published the following year. That was 18 years after the first book on skating in any language, Robert Jones's *Treatise on Skating*, was published. Jones's practical manual for beginning skaters who want to look good on the ice appeared in 1772 and was reprinted, sometimes with revisions, numerous times between then and 1855.* Vieth's book has enjoyed comparatively little fame despite being more interesting in some ways. It is more abstract than Jones': Vieth skips advice on skates in favor of describing the allure of the ice using Klopstock's poetry. Like Jones, Vieth tells his readers how to skate a spiral line, but unlike Jones, Vieth's discussion is explicitly grounded in physics. Jones covers more skating moves than Vieth, but Vieth emphasizes a connection to dance and is the first to suggest skating to music.

Despite its importance for understanding the earliest days of figure skating, Vieth's book was almost lost to skating history. This translation was inspired by a footnote. In *End of the Compulsories: A Remembrance*, James Hines writes,

---

*R. Jones and W. E. Cormack, *A Treatise on Skating*, ed. B. A. Thurber (Evanston, IL: Skating History Press, 2017).

> In 1790, just eighteen years after Robert Jones published his *Treatise* in London, Gerhard Ulrich Anton Vieth described a relatively high level of skating in Germany. His *Über das Schlittschuhlaufen* (About Skating), presented originally as a lecture in Dessau, was published in both Leipzig and Vienna.*

In the accompanying footnote, Hines admits, "This author has been unable to locate a copy of Vieth's book." I had been able to locate a scanned version in Google books some time earlier. It seemed like time to make Vieth's work readily available.†

Hines' trouble finding a copy may be due to a citation error nearly a century before he wrote that note. In that note, Hines says he knows about the book because Zindel includes it in his bibliography.‡ Zindel calls Vieth's book *Ueber das Schlittschuhlaufen*. Putting that into Google and the online library catalogs isn't much help because it's not quite right. Correct the title to *Ueber das Schrittschuhlaufen* and it comes right up.

Whether the correct German word for skating was *Schrittschuhlaufen* or *Schlittschuhlaufen* was a topic of debate in the eighteenth century. The former is the historically correct form: the *Schritt* comes from the verb

---

*James R. Hines, *End of the Compulsories: A Remembrance* (n.p.: Self-published, 2022), 34, 36.

†Sadly, Hines will never get to read Vieth. He passed away on September 7, 2022 ("Hines," *Skating* 99, no. 10 [December 2022]: 47).

‡Christian Siegmund Zindel, *Der Eislauf* (Nürnberg: Friedrich Campe, 1825), 78.

schreiten, which in today's German means "to stride." However, *schreiten* originally had a sliding connotation. Meissner* has argued that the "slide" meaning remained in Old High German using evidence from *Hildebrandslied*, which was written in the 830s, making it the earliest German poem. The meaning of the verb soon shifted in German, though cognates in other languages retain the "slide" meaning.

By the eighteenth century, interest in both etymology and skating led to lively debates about which word to use. Among the best-known discussions is one held by Goethe and Klopstock. Goethe described it in his autobiography:

> We spoke namely in good southern German of *Schlittschuhen*, which he did not accept as valid because the the word does not come from *Schlitten*, as if one puts on little runners, but rather from *Schreiten*, that is, one, like the Homeric gods, strides over the sea become a floor on winged shoes.†

As you'll soon see, Vieth was a huge fan of Klopstock, so naturally he used Klopstock's preferred spelling—*Schrittschuh*—in the title. By this point, however, ordinary people thought skating was more about little run-

---

*R. Meissner, "Zum Hildebrandslied," *Zeitschrift für deutsches Altertum und deutsche Literatur* N. F. 30 (= 42) (1898): 122–128.

†Erich Trunz, ed., *Goethes Werke: Hamburger Ausgabe in 14 Bänden*, vol. 9 (Hamburg: C. Wegner, 1948), III.61–62. My translation, previously published in Fowler, *On the Outside Edge*, 81.

ners than big strides, plus the *slide* meaning of *schreiten* had mostly been forgotten. *Schritt-* turned into *Schlitt-* as the word was reanalyzed. This is an example of folk etymology, where the seeminingly inappropriate "stride"-word was replaced by the more familiar "slide"-word.

The point of this etymological digression is that this book has been hard for skating historians to get hold of. Fowler's[*] comments on it are detailed enough to show that he read it:

> The first publication of importance [in Germany] is dated 1788, and is a lecture delivered to a club of friends in Dessau, by **G. U. A. Vieth**,[†] a lecturer on mathematics in that town. At this date skating in Germany was evidently behind that of England, but beginning to expand. The lecture is practically devoted to big curves and spirals of outside edge, interspersed with flights of rhetoric and long quotations from Klopstock. At the end Vieth refers to further "artificialities," but dismisses them somewhat contemptuously, citing only the **OF** loop **3**, the earliest mention of a loop **3** in literature.

Fowler is one of the few skating historians to write in English who have actually read Vieth. George Hel-

---

[*]Fowler, *On the Outside Edge*, 60–61.

[†]G. U. A. Vieth: Neue Litteratur und Völkerkunde (1789), pp. 100-126. (Leipzig.) *[Note in Fowler.]*

frich, who mainly wrote in German, quotes one of Vieth's comments on women in this book (page 26) and his general opinion on women skating (he approved, to some extent; see page 30) in an article translated for *Skating* in 1926.[*] Hines[†] remarks that Nigel Brown "apparently did locate a copy of [Vieth] but provides minimal information about it." In fact, Brown[‡] doesn't include any details beyond what Fowler wrote. It's unclear whether he actually had access to a copy before 1959.

Today, it's easy to get hold of Vieth's book online as long as you search for the correct title, but the fact that it is in German is a barrier to some readers. This translation makes Vieth's important work readily available to a new generation of skating historians.

---

[*]George Helfrich, "Henriette Sontag," trans. Mrs. William Amory, *Skating*, May 1926, 39–41.

[†]Hines, *End of the Compulsories: A Remembrance*, 36, n. 50.

[‡]Nigel Brown, *Ice-Skating: A History* (London: Nicholas Kaye Limited, 1959), 49–50.

Vieth's life and work

Gerhard Ulrich Anton Vieth was born on January 8, 1763 in Hooksiel, Lower Saxony, Germany, on the coast of the North Sea just west of the Netherlands.*

Vieth was the second of eleven children born to magistrate Julius Christoph Vieth (1731–1795) and Conradina Augusta Gerdes (1742–1794) and the first to survive to adulthood—his older brother, Gerhard Georg, lived just four days, from August 18 to August 22, 1761. Four of Vieth's younger siblings made it to adulthood:

- Sophia Catharina (1765–1836)
- Susanna Margerita Christiana (1770–1825)
- Aegidius Conrad (1772–1811)
- August Julius (1773–1842)

Four, in addition to Gerhard Georg, weren't so lucky:

- Susanna Margaretha Christiana (1766–1768)

---

*Unless otherwise noted, the information about Vieth's family is based on the family tree on FamilySearch (www.familysearch.org), where Vieth's personal identification code is KZTF-YZT. Credit is due to emilyleonard323 and Erin Duerichen Strand for their work assembling it. Much of the detail on Vieth's family comes from a report assembled by professional geneaologist Ernst Vierthaler for Friedrich Duerichen in the early 1960s. Vieth's page is dated August 28, 1960. Strand has kindly made the report available on FamilySearch. The remaining information is from the collection "Germany, Lutheran Baptisms, Marriages, and Burials, 1500–1971" (or, in German, "Deutschland, ausgewählte evangelische Kirchenbücher 1500–1971"), which is searchable via *FamilySearch*.

Figure 1: Portrait of Gerhard Ulrich Anton Vieth from his chapter on skating in *Das gesammte Turnwesen*.

- Georg Julius (1768–1775)
- Johann Georg (1778–1880)
- Franciskus (1781–1781)

The lifespans of the remaining sibling, Conradine Auguste (b. 1779) is unclear; I could not find a record of her death. It is likely that she, too, died in childhood.

Vieth grew up in Hookseil, a small town off the coast of the North Sea in the Wilhelmshaven area of German East Frisia.* The area featured a network of canals, making it perfect for a young skater. As a boy, he was gifted with unusual strength and agility. He channeled these talents into fencing, dancing, vaulting, and horseback riding.†

In 1781, he went to the University of Göttingen; two years later, he moved to the University of Leipzig to continue his studies in mathematics, physics, and law. He remained there until 1786, when he accepted a position teaching mathematics and French at the new Hauptschule in Dessau, which is just north of Leipzig. Outside of school hours, he tutored students in fencing and geometry. In 1799, Vieth became the school's director.‡

---

*A map of Hookseil in 1893 can be found at http://www.deutschefotothek.de/documents/obj/71052436.
Due to copyright restrictions it could not be reproduced here, but the online version's zoom capabilities make it more attractive anyway.

†C. Euler, "Vieth, Gerhard Ulrich Anton," *Allgemeine Deutsche Biographie* 38 (1895): 682–684, https://www.deutsche-biographie.de/sfz83762.html.

‡Euler.

On April 5, 1793, Vieth married Dorothea Henriette Sophie Beibler (January 25, 1770–May 1, 1827). They had eleven children:

1. Johanne Christiane Luise (b. January 15, 1793— three months before his parents' marriage!)
2. Julius Carl Eberhard (b. April 16, 1794)
3. Karl August (December 26, 1795–April 6, 1814)
4. Heinrich Friedrich Konrad (September 27, 1707– August 17, 1798)
5. Elisabeth Henriette (July 18, 1799–July 8, 1838)
6. Eduard Justus (b. March 9, 1801)
7. Auguste Caroline (December 28, 1802–December 15, 1875)
8. Heinrich Friedrich (b. December 12, 1804)
9. Hermann Anton (July 30, 1809–October 11, 1864)
10. Wilhelm Theodor (August 22, 1810–September 24, 1810)
11. Victor Ludwig (b. January 21, 1812)

Like Vieth's siblings, few of his children survived to adulthood. Vierthaler's report provides birthdays for all eleven, but only dates of death for six. Of the other five, I was able to track down the futures of three whose marriages are recorded in the German church records available via *FamilySearch*:

1. Julius Carl Eberhard married Dorothea Caroline Auguste Buschow (b. 1798) on June 25, 1819, in Berlin.
2. Eduard Justus married Antonie Friederike Emme Fritze (b. 1816) on May 26, 1835, in Berlin.

3. Victor Ludwig married Mathilde Junker (b. 1820) on February 28, 1850, in Prussia.

The futures of Johanne Christiane Luise and Heinrich Friedrich remain unknown. It is likely that they died in childhood.

As a professional educator, Vieth is best known for his stance on physical education. He called "a healthy soul in a healthy body" the "great purpose every educational institution must work towards" in a speech at the fiftieth anniversary of his school in Dessau.* His *Versuch einer Encyklopädie der Leibesübungen* in two volumes, published in 1794 and 1795, stands alongside Johann Christoph Friedrich GutsMuths, *Gymnastik für die Jugend: Enthaltend eine praktische Anweisung zu Leibesübungen* (Schnepfenthal: Buchhandlung der Erziehungsanstalt, 1793) and Friedrich Ludwig Jahn and Ernst Eiselen, *Die deutsche Turnkunst zur Einrichtung der Turnplätze* (Berlin: Self-published, 1816) as one of the great German works on physical education.

Vieth's wife Dorothea died on May 1, 1826, leaving Vieth depressed both "physically and mentally."[†] After a long illness, he died on January 12, 1836, at age 73. He is buried in the Historischer Friedhof (historic cemetary) in Dessau.[‡] Monuments have been erected in his memory in Hookseil and Dessau.

---

*Euler, "Vieth, Gerhard Ulrich Anton."
[†]Euler.
[‡]Historische Friedhof I, Dessau, Stadtkreis Dessau-Roßlau, Sachsen-Anhalt, Germany, s.v. "Gerhard Ulrich Anton Vieth," *FindAGrave.com*. Find a Grave Memorial ID 201770260.

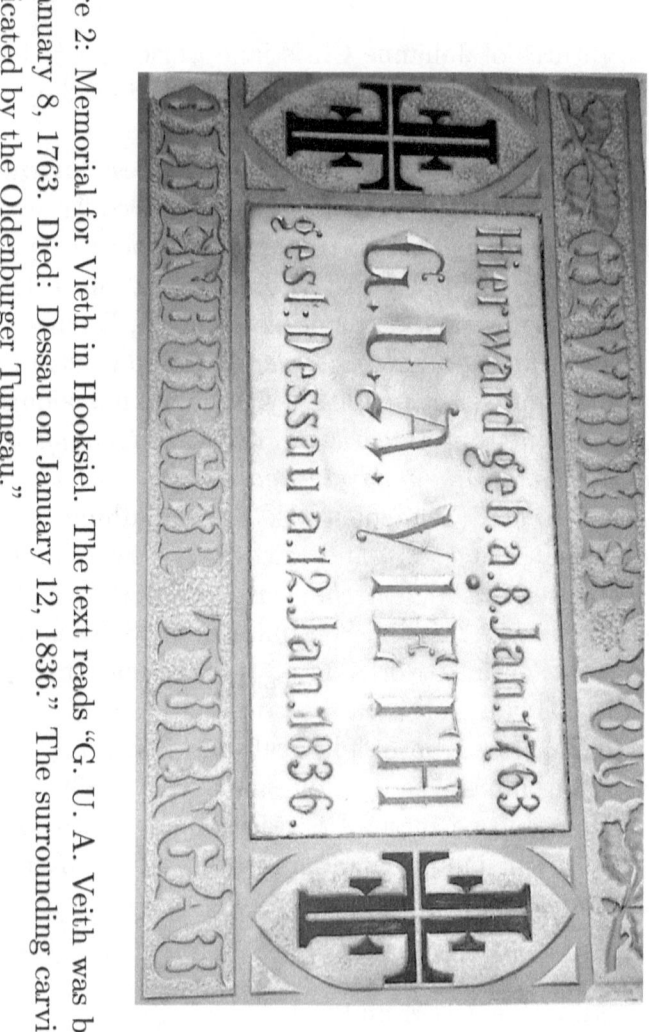

Figure 2: Memorial for Vieth in Hooksiel. The text reads "G. U. A. Veith was born here on January 8, 1763. Died: Dessau on January 12, 1836." The surrounding carving reads "Dedicated by the Oldenburger Turngau."

Figure 3: Memorial for Vieth in Dessau. The text reads "Gerhard Ulrich Anton Vieth, January 8, 1763 – January 12, 1836. The pioneer of physical education. Erected 1963."

Translator's note

This translation is based on the book published in 1790, which was based on the transcript of a lecture Vieth gave in Dessau in 1788. The text of the lecture was published in *Neue Litteratur und Völkerkunde* the following year. The book adds a foreword by an anonymous editor, a few notes (designated as additions in the present volume), and the full text of three poems by Friedrich Gottlieb Klopstock: "Der Eislauf" (Skating, 1764), "Braga" (1766), and "Die Kunst Tialfs" (Tialf's Art, 1767). Vieth's text is the same in the article and book versions.

Instead of trying to translate Klopstock's poetry, I have simply quoted William Nind's translations, which were published in 1848. Like many poetic translations, they rework the originals instead of rendering them literally in the new language. Nind's version have the benefit of being reasonably close to Vieth chronologically. They provide a sense of what contemporary English speakers (or at least, English speakers not as temporally removed as we are) would have admired in Klopstock's poetry. I have followed Vieth and Nind in spelling the names of characters from Old Norse mythology in the main text and given more modern versions in notes.

Figures 4–7 were originally published in the 1789 version. They are based on versions digitized by Google Books. I have cleaned them up by removing the background and relabeling the points Vieth refers to for clarity. There were no captions in either of the original publications. The ones included here are my additions. The endnotes (identified by numbers in the text) are also my additions and can be found starting on page 65. Footnotes are identified by symbols and appear, with a note as to whether they are from the 1789 or 1790 edition, at the bottom of each page.

On Skating

Foreword

The present treatise on skating was presented at a society of friends on March 1, 1788 in Dessau. The author of this excellent work is G. U. A. Vieth. An aficionado of this art intends to make a pleasant gift to his friends by reprinting it from the popular monthly magazine of Mr. von Archenholz, *Neue Litteratur und Völkerkunde*, because this journal is not widely distributed here in the countryside.

The new editor subscribes with pleasure to all the sentiments of the author and rejoices that this art has found a man who could so thoroughly develop its theory and so enchantingly portray the charms and pleasures it affords. As far as is known, nobody has yet systematized skating, nor, aside from the current work, described it as an art.

Indisputibly, the northern peoples have come a long way in this respect, and one must admire their courage and skill. Nevertheless, there are still a few points, especially in regard to beauty, that could be applied to ice skating. Why shouldn't skating be raised to the rank of a fine art alongside its older sister, dance? But who, more competent judges, dares to anticipate this apotheosis?

It is sad that this art must have been unknown to the southern Greeks because of its nature. A nation that knew how to infuse so much grace into all its arts and how to put the type of philosophy that always leads to perfection into every thing would have derived great charm and pleasure from it!

There are few types of exercise that give an enthusiast so much enjoyment as this one without wearing them out. Dance, riding, swimming, ... demand more effort. If our bodies become excited through pleasant movement that is effortless, gentle, and fast, then skating surely deserves first place. Only a skillful edge-runner can describe the inexpressible pleasure found in the wavy curves as he creates circles on the ice.

Another advantage must not be forgotten: this art is based on consistent, even mathematical, principles. The skater therefore enjoys the most uninterrupted pleasure and is completely the master of the movement. He can make his run as fast, smooth, graceful, ... as he wants to, once he possesses the requisite skill and dexterity.

The current editor originally wanted to use his own recollections and experiences of skating and to share various practical rules for learning and practicing the art in comments. However, the notes would have outgrown the text. Perhaps time will offer another opportunity for that.

Beginners have the most difficulty. Fear and terror overpower them when they see an artist floating along as if in the air, with incomprehensible speed, supported by almost nothing. The fear of falling and the lack of trust in their skill deprive most beginners of the pleasure that they do not yet know. Courage is required for every physical exercise; skating no more than riding, swimming, ... If a beginner holds his body bent forward, as if he were about to sit down, he is never in danger of falling backwards. Any other fall can be broken by the hands,[1] and can only be harmful if he doesn't give into it at the right time and tries to regain his balance by force by flailing with his arms. The hands are thereby removed from the place where they are most needed to support the falling body.

Once the beginner has overcome this difficulty, he has gained a great deal. Moreover, if he has a guide who will acquaint him with the theory and give him the necessary practical instruction, he can easily reach the point at which the exercise becomes pleasant in a short time.

Above all, the key to this, as to all arts and skills in the world, is:

Natura facit habilem, ars facilem ususque potentem.[2]

Graz, January 1, 1790.

Skating

If any subject can claim to be discussed in our meetings, it is certainly the one that I have the honor of attempting to present to you today.[3] Is it necessary to convince us of the importance of skating? Or is it not simply enough to say that nearly all of us, including me, have ranked it at the top of our lists of favorite pastimes? Wasn't it always one of the most excellent physical exercises, which was given only to the more robust North and is unknown in the cushy southern lands? Wouldn't Homer and Virgil, who could not paint the light, floating gaits of their deities as they appeared and disappeared beautifully enough, believe that Apollo and the Muses, appearing to their astounded eyes in philanthropic guise, if they arose from their graves or urns and could take a look at the frozen Stilling?* And as for the German who is Homer and Pindar combined[4]—didn't he dedicate some of his most beautiful odes to this noble art, of which he himself is a master? Is there a better a better way to strengthen the entire body that connects clean air with rapid play of the muscles? Outside of it, is there a better way to prompote the *motum peristalticum*[5] or increase the appetite? Who doesn't feel an increased elasticity in all the fibers during such a more-than-earthly run? Who does not feel a kind of delight when the effects of weight and friction, which otherwise allow only

---
*A pond near Dessau. *[Note in original.]*

slow body movements, seem to stop, and he is able to fly away with lightning speed in attitudes that are only possible for an ice skater?

And afterward—can you name any weariness that could be sweeter or more comfortable as when we rest after skating? It is similar to something we know, if not from experience, then from Ovid's and Wieland's[6] charming descriptions! People praise May and its flowers, and the grapes of fall, but when do they provide such a great source of pleasure as a merry December day? When have we seen so much true charm on the promenade, where such aspiring grace is exhibited, as in the swaying of ice skating?

Don't people praise loud, glittering balls with their laughter and witticism? When—to believe Klopstock— did Nossa, the goddess of grace,[7] show us more? In the coy, scurrying, and bouncing antics of the shoes of young fops, who we see dancing cotillons on two or (in the new fashion) one leg? Or in the manly, wide-ranging curves of ice skates?[8]

And now take what gives everything else the greatest charm and is lacking here: a soft, plump girl, wrapped in warm, silky furs in a light, dainty sled, which you make fly before you, with her as if on the wings of the wind down the mirror-bright track, and be rewarded for this sweet effort with an even sweeter smile! I wish you just one experience like the one I've described here, from my youth, in case you have never done anything similar. Then you would agree with me that a good ice surface, under the right circumstances, is better than all the dance halls in the world. I can still imagine the motley row of sleds as we skated down a canal to the port of Jeverland a mile from the town on the sea![9] I can still see the truly enchanting sight of the masts of the ships, just barely visible, quickly emerging from the blue distance as the shore and the city flew from us!

> We, fleet as thought, through widening circles sway,
> As waves the sea-snake in mid ocean lost.
>
> Klopstock[10]

Now I hear the lively din of the rink, the happy jokes, and the songs of society! — But where to?

Forgive this wool-gathering, gentlemen! Who doesn't have scenes from the past linked to almost every analogous situation in the present? A cowherd's song transports a person from Switzerland to the romantic banks of the Aare. Similarly, I can't stop soaring on the excellent surface of the Hookseiler Tief[11] in my homeland when talking about ice skating.

What a pity, forever a pity! that we know no more of the history of an invention that affords so many delights to the enthusiast.

> SUNK in the tomb of endless night
>   Lies many a great inventor's name:
> Our torch we kindle at their light;
>   But where is their reward of fame?

How mane ye him, who ocean cross'd
>   First with tall mast and swelling sheet?
> I would not e'en his name were lost
>   Who added wings to flying feet.
>
> For should he not immortal live,
>   Whose art can health and joy enhance,
> Such as no nettled steed can give,
>   Such, e'en, as pants not in the dance?

Klopstock[12]

Some, however, seems certain, and it is already clear from the nature of the climate that the peoples of the North were the first to make this discovery.[13] According to their old mythology, it is descended from Braga[14] himself, the famous god of poetry, Valhalla's singer. Klopstock has him sing this:

> To heroes* in the sacred wood
>
> My songs, and Bard and Scald with fire inform,
> I—sound it, Telyn, to the Hebrus!—I
> Invented these, the wingèd shaft and storm,
>   In race victorious to outvie.

Klopstock[15]

---

*The heroes in Valhall. *[Note in original.]*

Uller, the son of Siphia, a half-god whose attributes are beauty, arrows, and skates; Tialf, a companion of Thor; and Harold, a king of the North, are cited as his students.[16] Because of the second, ice skating is called Tialf's art in the language of our native Homer.[17] Nossa, who is called the most beautiful of the goddesses by the bards and skalds whenever they want to express charm and grace, became, as is easily imagined, known as a great friend and protector of the ice.

Perhaps the bards once sang suitable songs, as might be inferred from the expressions "dance of the bards" and "bardic dance song," if they were in old poems. However much value our ancestors placed on the skill of skating, it is already clear that they made gods into its inventors and goddesses into its protectors. Another confirmation is given by a song of the aforementioned Nordic King Harold, in which this favorite of Nossa laments the cruelty of his beloved:

> I fight with courage. I keep a firm seat on horseback. I am skilled in swimming. I glide along the ice on scates. I excell in darting the lance. ... And yet a Russian maid disdains me.[18]

Would that a better connoisseur of ancient history than I might succeed in discovering traces in our society from which the origin and the gradual development of this bold invention could be traced.

In the modern world, the people living along the northern coast of Germany and Holland are known as the best skaters. Among them, the boatmen especially excite admiration, partly for the boldness of their curves and partly for their almost unbelievable swiftness. Their bodies, accustomed to strong and fast movements by working on ships, control their own power in every position, no matter how daring, and remain balanced with the greatest ease. They are divided into two types, edge-runners and shovers.[19] The former make grace their goal, the latter speed, and the latter get their name because they are often used to push ladies' sleds.*

I know among them some, who made a round trip of two miles at least four times per day.[20] It used to be more common than it is now for women to put on skates. Dutch women still do it most often, and indeed it is hardly possible to imagine more grace than in the soft, light movements of a skating girl, who seems to move like a goddess on a crystal plane.[21] The edge-runners make a study of the beauty of the positions

---

*There is one more type of skating. One does not lift either foot, but still travels quickly. The motion is brought about by continuously shifting the weight of the body from one foot to the other and pushing the body forward with an imperceptible pressure with the foot without the body weight. The drawing below shows the progression from A to B. The light lines indicate the pressure of the pushing foot, while the weight of the body is imperceptibly transferred to the skating foot.

So-called skating through great leaps, the way people run on the ground, is a bastard and does not deserve notice because of its violent and shapeless motion. *[Note added in the 1790 republication.]*

and motion. The skating professor in Göttingen,[22] who was only a bungler compared with some of the shippers, gave the necessary instruction for a fair honorarium *praenumerando*[23];—I would always rank him ahead of the English boxing professors, who charge 1/2 Reichsthaler for a lesson.[24]

The rules of good skating are fairly similar to those of good dancing, and may be reduced to the following principles:

1. The head must be held straight, just like nature intends, with a slight inclination towards the shoulder on the side you lean towards.

2. The back must necessarily remain stiff, because otherwise the center of gravity could move at any moment, and it would be impossible to support it consistently.

3. One of the main ornaments is the beautiful form of the curve described by the skating foot. It shouldn't be too short, meaning it doesn't have to curve too tightly, because then the movement of the body becomes more rocking than balanced. An extended curve is obtained by not putting the skating foot down too soon. This must happen at the very moment when the other foot has completed the previous stroke and is about to give the final impulse.[25] It must be quite close to the other; furthermore, if, e.g., the right foot is on the ice, pull the left shoulder back and push the right one forward, and in this position the body leans forward in a straight line.

4. The swing of the free leg is key. As we shall soon see, this is very important for skating. The error of swinging the foot forward quickly and immediately after the thrust has been made, and making this swing high in the air, is very common because few have enough aesthetic feeling to want to avoid arousing admiration by forced, violent, and excessive movements. It is very offensive to the connoisseur of true beauty. In contrast, just as a Vestris[26] beats his *entrechat*[27] as low as possible, so also the true skater, following rules similar to Noverre's,[28] swings the carelessly lifted foot with the toe down close to the ice with a delicate twist after initially holding it somewhat behind behind the skating foot.

5. Above all, it is a general rule, both in ballet and in bardic dance,[29] to draw the feet together (*effaçer*) as much as possible while balancing, by means of which

6. the knees, though not stiff like stilts, do not need to be bent as much as the shovers do to promote speed.

7. The seventh rule is inherent in the stroke of the edge-runner, namely, that the last thrust of the foot that is being lifted should be done diagonally, i.e., half backwards and half sideways, because changing the lean of the body to the other side and forwards is only possible under these circumstances. Without it, the line of skating will not remain in the correct direction.

8–9. The eighth and ninth rules are two requirements that Noverre gives for a good dancer that are just as indispensable to the good edge-runner: to allow the thighs to rotate outwards, and to be firm in the loins. Here they are, in the famous dancer's own words, from his *Letters on Dance*, letter 12.[30]

> [In order to dance well, Sir,] nothing is so important as the turning outwards of the thigh; and nothing is so natural to men as the contrary position. ... A dancer with his limbs turned inwards is awkward and disagreeable. The contrary attitude gives ease and brilliancy, it invests steps, positions and attitudes with grace. (117, 118)
>
> Further: One cannot be an excellent dancer without being firm in the loins, even if one possess all the other qualities essential to the perfection of this art... [When the ribs are weak,] it is impossible to maintain oneself perpendicularly ... the weakness of that part of the body is inimical to *aplomb* and equilibrium. ... Being deflected from its centre of gravity, [the body] only regains its equilibrium after contortions which are inconsistent with the graceful and harmonious movements of dancing. (126)

10. The carriage of the arms is nothing less than neu-

tral. Here, however, the rules of the ice surface deviate from the laws of the dance floor. A *port de bras*,[31] necessary for social and even more for theatrical dance, if I exclude the English solo, would have a very adverse effect in the dance of Tialf's apprentices, at least as it is now. Here the arms must somehow rest against the body and be still. Crossing the arms carelessly, or putting one hand on the chest and the other in the pocket of the coat—but never higher than the shoulders—may be the best position in this respect, because then there is the greatest semblance of lightness and carelessness, insofar as the latter word means the opposite of exertion, and also because the center of gravity thereby obtains its correct permanent position. It is located higher in the body, which all facilitates the free sweeping motion. In contrast, the arms, as soon as they are set free, fall into a rowing motion that, because of the nature of the changing movements of the feet the posture, is too natural a motion for the beginner not to have a hard time breaking the habit. It is far less offensive to the eye when walking than it is when skating. The reason for this is as clear as day.

11. Impetuous speed is never compatible with beauty, as our own feelings had certainly told us long before we heard Platner or read the writings of Burke, Hogarth, and other connoisseurs.[32] This then is the last rule for true apprentices of Tialf: We will never—for we do not want to sacrifice

beauty for speed—be among those "who loved flying steel,"[33] except in the event that we do a favor for a beauty sitting in a sled. But why don't I take the words of the honored poet, with whose stanzas I have already embellished, or rather darkened, my essay? Here is the beginning of the excellent bardic song, in which Bliid,[34] Haining, and Wandor sing of Tialf's art. Bliid begins to his companion Haining—

BLIID.

How rings the ice! Stay thy impetuous feet!
　　The night-breath glimmers o'er the frozen seas!
Still on thou speedest! From a course too fleet
　　Affrighted NOSSA flees.

HAINING.

She follows after. I in rhythmic dance
　　O'ertake the shaft fresh-wingèd from the bow.
How the smooth plain resounds to my advance!
　　Is NOSSA's foot too slow?

BLIID.

Provoke her not, o'ertaker of the reed!
　　Scorn'd she returns no more. I see it now,
Her anger is begun: hold in thy speed!
　　The cloud is on her brow.

HAINING.

> Dost see them by the rock come down the lake
> In the clear air of bright December morn?
> How they wave onward! Dearly will I take
> Revenge of Hlyda's scorn.

—I'll stop there, gentlemen. I can hardly resist the temptation to transcribe the whole poem. Who would endure the monotony of a lecture when the *Allehand** of one of Klopstock's poems fills the soul!

The above may be an imperfect theory of practicing skating, but perhaps it is worth a more detailed treatment. Let me add just one more thing:

Rhythm is the most excellent tool for perfecting any regular movement; this is proven not only by the ballroom but also by tightrope walkers and vaulters, for whom music is indispensable as it gives their dangerous movements and the gallop of their horses the necessary definite measure.[35] Skating is already a rich source of pleasure — but what could it become if music fit the long lines of beauty, merged with it, and, through the beat and soaring melody, enlivened the swing of steel. Better and faster the beginner would learn, and the master would surpass himself. Imagine what a feeling!

---

*The complete harmony of a poem. *[Note in original.]*

On Skating

At the heart-lifting sound of the horns, to sway blissfully as if on air, like spirits wrapped in ethereal bodies, floating on clouds!

Leaving this prospect of a future embellished skating, I turn to the closer consideration of this movement, insofar as it is a subject of mathematical and physical investigation. For the friend of the sublime science that chiefly bears this name, every new application of it to real-life situations that he has the opportunity to experience daily has immense charm. If the object itself is pleasure, like what we have here, then that attraction is doubled.

Some of the fundamental laws of motion will assist us in discussing the case of skating.[36]

1. The first is the law of inertia: Any body set in motion by any force moves with the same velocity and in the same direction until a new force acts upon it, compelling it to change its direction or velocity or inhibiting its motion completely. This new force may be mere resistance, such as that which arises from friction. Although most of the movements we perceive cease very soon because resistance occurs in almost all of them, the law just quoted is just as obvious to the reflective mind as that which experience constantly confirms: that a body at rest remains still until a force sets it in motion.

2. The second is the law according to which conspiring forces act on a body. Namely: when two forces act on a body in such a way that their di-

rections are at an angle, they cancel something out in one another and force the body to take a middle direction. This direction is found by making a parallelogram from the two forces, the magnitude and direction of which can be very easily expressed by lines, with the appropriate angle and drawing its diagonal, which is the central direction required. The proof of that does not belong here.[37] The more obtuse the angle between the two directions of force is, the more one counteracts the other, or the more one cancels out the other, the smaller their overall effect must be, that is, the smaller the mean direction must be.

3. In every heavy body there is a point around which the mass of the body is always equally distributed in two opposite directions. This point is called the center of mass or the center of gravity. If this point is supported, then the whole body is supported and secure. However, a body may be supported at other points. If the perpendicular line from the center of gravity to the horizontal plane[38] does not pass through the base of the support, but is outside it, then the body falls. The center of gravity must therefore be taken into account when moving the body.*

---

*Merely by transferring the center of gravity from one foot to the other, the skating foot can obtain so much propulsion that it is unnecessary to push with the other foot—unless you are looking for grace or good skating.

Skillful skaters know how to combine throwing the center of gravity while simultaneously trasferring it from one foot to the

It is also noteworthy that the center of gravity (which is most commonly found by sliding an object back and forth on a straight edge, like that of a triangular prism)[39] in the human body is in the region of the navel.

4. If a body moves in a crooked line, there is certainly more than one force: there must be forces in different directions (conspiring forces) acting on it. It is true that these can also occur with straight-line motion. But when one force constantly drives a body towards a fixed point, while the other pushes it sideways away from that point, the movement need not become crooked. A push from the hand of the Almighty, which drives a planet sideways from its sun, and the constant pull of gravity from that very sun, together with the law of inertia, cause the planet to swing about in an eternal orbit. Central forces, that is, centripetal and centrifugal forces (the expressions are self-explanatory) are therefore necessary for curved motion.

5. A falling body falls with accelerated motion. Our plan does not require mentioning which law this is according to.

Now, with the above as a basis, let me try to apply it to our subject.

---

other by pushing, so that they are able to give their run the greatest speed with the least effort. *[Note added in the 1790 republication.]*

We must use the previous division into straight and curved skating to continue our discussion from that one to this one, that is, from the easier to the more difficult.

In fig. 4, which I have the honor of presenting to you here, a shover travels in a straight line. The body leans so far forwards that the center of gravity, G, is in front of the skater's base. That base is very small—only the short area in which the blade on the skating foot, B, touches the ice. Since line from the center of gravity perpendicular to the ice surface, GE, does not touch this line, the body is supposed to fall. It would, if foot B remained in one place. Then the center of gravity G would indisputibly sink down along arc GD, along which the radius GB remains the same. This sinking is prevented by the force of the other foot, R, through which the body is driven in direction BD at the very moment at which the center of gravity should sink. It should fall at any moment, but at every moment it must stay in the same position because of the motion of foot B.

From this it is clear: the more the center of gravity is inclined, that is, the farther the body leans forward, the faster it should fall and therefore, the faster foot B must travel and the stronger the free foot R must push. Repeated practice teaches the skater to measure, with admirable accuracy, the amount of thrust necessary for any inclination of the body and conversely, the lean of the body necessary for every intensity of thrust. If there is a mismatch here, an insecure position, staggering, or even falling is an inevitable consequence. If the lean were too strong for the thrust, the tobacco-

Figure 4: Skating in a straight line.

pipe and the nose would be in the greatest danger, and if the thrust were too much for the lean, another part of the body would soon sit down very roughly. The strength of the thrust, and consequently the extent of the lean, soon finds its limits, not only because of the muscles of the calf and thigh but also because a very strong thrust requires a very strong lean, implying a very oblique position of the body. Consequently, it would have to be done at such a small angle to the ice surface that its effect would be lost. The steel would not be able to grip the ice securely enough, but would slip. The inclination could therefore probably not be made much greater than the figure indicates, because then the thrust with foot R would not be strong enough to match the amount of lean.

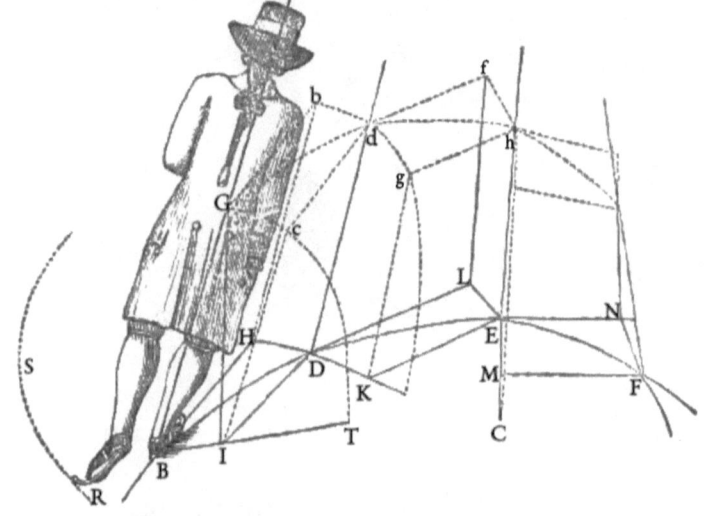

Figure 5: Skating on a curve.

Nobody can actually skate as straight as I have described here, because the pushing foot must always be placed a little bit sideways, so that the edge of the steel can press against the ice. This is why the body receives a little push to the side. But we can ignore this here; otherwise, we would have to assume a sideways lean for the center of gravity, and this case is treated later, when it becomes more noticable.

Now to the sweep of the edge-runner in fig. 5. That his path is curved is clear from experience; this must be caused by central forces. We divide the path into different elements with the same time interval, e.g., instants,[40] in the order of the letters BDEF.

At the beginning of the first instant, foot R gave the

body, with center of gravity G, a push in direction Gb in such a way that the center of gravity G would only have to pass through space Gb in the first instant by virtue of this push. But the edge-runner simultaneously leans his body strongly to the side towards C,[41] and the line from the center of gravity perpendicular to the ground, GI, falls far beyond the support point B in the horizontal plane. Therefore, G must fall along arc GT. Suppose this happens, and it reaches c in the first instant. Here we have a compound motion of the center of gravity: one through Gb because of the push and the other through Gc because of the fall at the same time. If we make the parallelogram of the forces whose direction and magnitude are expressed by the lines mentioned, it follows that the center of gravity must move along the diagonal line Gd in the first instant. Therefore, Gd is the first element of the center of gravity's trajectory.

In spite of this, foot B could just follow the push to BH, so that at the end of the first instant it would be at H, while the center of gravity would be at d. However, the body would be unable to maintain this very crooked position and would fall sideways—something that often occurs with beginners in edge-running. Once made wise by experience, they soon learn to turn the whole body and the skating foot[42] in the direction we have just determined for the center of gravity. The correct swing of the free foot[43] R through arc RS helps tremendously. Through this swing, the body is put in the correct position without effort, so that in the first instant, the skating foot, B, describes a diagonal, BD, similar to the above.

Now we are at the beginning of the second instant and are looking for the necessary power again.

The centrifugal force, which was the first impulse a moment ago, is now found from the law of inertia. The body (both the center of gravity and the foot) had direction Gd; BD at the end of the first instant. By virtue of the law of inertia, it will continue in this direction with the same speed. The center of gravity will therefore travel along line df in the second instant, and likewise the foot will travel along line DL.

Again, the centripetal force on the center of gravity causes its tendency to fall. Because the body made the necessary turn during the first instant, the direction in which it will fall must necessarily be towards C, just as before, so that the center of gravity will now fall along dg.

In this way the directions of the two central forces are found. However, their magnitudes have not remained the same as in the first instant, but have undergone the following changes:

- The centrifugal force is considerably reduced by the friction of the skate on the ice.

- In contrast, the centripetal force on the center of gravity has been increased proportionally. It could perhaps be said to have increased by itself, because bodies that are sinking or falling have accelerated motion. I doubt, however, whether this law can be applied here, because the center of gravity during the first instant, despite its efforts to fall, does not actually get any lower; at every smallest instant the skating foot brings it into the previous position by following it. Moreover, it cannot be denied that this centripetal force becomes smaller and smaller, for we see that the edge-runner has the strongest lean at the beginning of his arc. As he glides, he gradually straightens up with the help of his free foot, so that he stands upright again at the end of the arc. It is self-evident that otherwise falling would be inevitable. However, this decrease in the centripetal force is not nearly as great as that of the centrifugal force caused by friction. The latter must necessarily be very strong, because the sharp steel blade cuts into the ice due to its oblique position, and moreover, because of the curved path, it must turn on the ice.

It is always true that, relative to each other, the centrifugal force gradually decreases and the centripetal force increases.

Therefore, df must be drawn much smaller for the second instant than Gb was drawn for the first instant, but dg for the second instant must be only a little smaller than Gc was for the first second (how much this change amounts to is far too complex). If we now draw the parallelogram of the forces dfhg and draw its diagonal dh, then the latter is the second element of the center of gravity's path. The path of the body, and consequently the trajectory of the skating foot, helped by the swinging movement of foot R, is the same as in the first instant.

In the same way, the other elements of the path can be found, for the third and following instants, constantly taking into account the fact that the centrifugal force constantly becomes smaller compared to the centripetal force, regardless of the fact that the latter also decreases in absolute terms.

However, from this last consideration it is sufficiently clear that the center of gravity G, and consequently the skating foot, B, following it, must come closer to C at the end of each subsequent second. The trajectory of the edge-runner is therefore a spiral line, as fig. 6 shows schematically: the faster decrease in the lines Af, Bf, Df, Ef, etc., which represent the centrifugal force, and the slower decreases in the centripetal force Ap, Bp, Dp, Ep, etc., catch the eye until they both reach C = 0. It is part of the edge-runner's art to cause both to become equal to zero at the same time, because the path will be unsteady if this is not the case.

If one allows the centripetal force of the center of gravity to decrease more quickly by trying to bring the body back to perpendicular too soon, as beginners tend to do out of timidity, decrease of the centrifugal force than would take place automatically is required. This can then only be brought about by significantly increasing the friction by allowing the sharp rear corner of the blade to scratch into the ice. If this is not done, the arc that was started will soon become a partially straight but irregular line. On the contrary, if some of the cen-

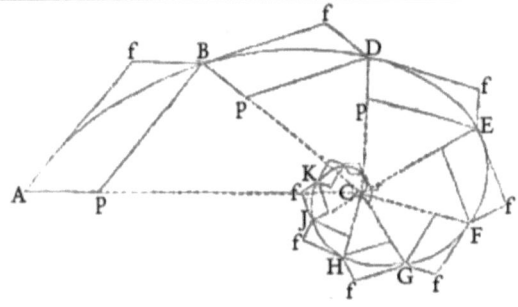

Figure 6: The spiral line created by a skater.

tripetal force still remains after the centrifugal force has already become equal to zero, then expect either anxious and uncomfortable gripping with the hands in an attempt to find a stable point for the center of gravity, or, in those who know how to help themselves a little better, the free foot to step over the skating foot, which is not entirely compatible with beauty and causes the remaining centripetal force to suddenly and somewhat violently be made equal to zero. Such sudden transitions are never graceful, and in this case there is still a danger of getting the skates entangled when stepping over, in which case the whole body plays a very sorry role. But these mistakes are as common to the beginner as wobbling at the center of gravity, which always results in a zigzag path. The master's perfection in the art of continuing the spiral line according to the law of continuity, by letting the two forces decrease harmoniously with one another, is only the work of long practice without rushing combined with temerity.

In the second and third figures, the diagonals themselves are drawn curved, which is justified because a change of direction happens at every smallest moment.

I pass over the other tricks that can be done on skates, partly because practicing them is not advisable because of the danger connected with some of them, and partly because they never have as much real beauty as the spiral movement. Among the best of these is, for example, the figure of a written Latin E. A quick look shows that the narrow middle narrow curve requires a violent swing if there is to be power left over for the last arc.[44]

A large repertoire of other movements that do not actually satisfy our purpose can follow the previous consideration of the spiral movement. I venture to mention only two of them briefly here, so that I do not abuse the attention you have been so good as to give to my subject.

We also find this spiral movement when we tilt a round disc (e.g., a coin or a hoop) slightly to the side and roll it forward in direction BM, as in fig. 7. The forces that cause the spiral movement of the center of gravity G here are the same as in the case of the edge-runner, but with the difference (which also serves to confirm the above remark) that here, the centripetal force on the center of gravity becomes stronger and stronger, and the disc finally falls with a whirling movement. However, the fact that the edge of the disc or point B (as the instantaneous contact point is called when the disc rolls away) follows a similar line can be easily explained by the fact that point n on the edge of

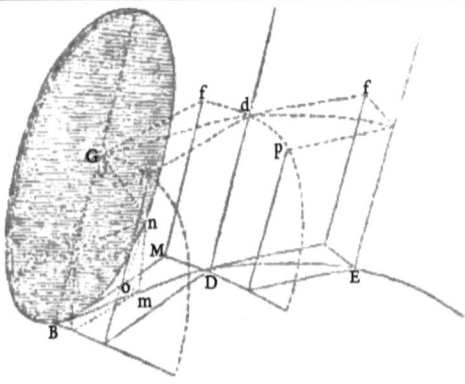

Figure 7: A coin rolling on a curve

the disc already overhangs line BM a little because of the disc's inclination. (This happened with the edge-runner through the conscious turning of the body and the swing of the free foot.) Therefore, when point n becomes point B as the disc rolls away (i.e., when point n touches the ground), it is no longer on line BM approximately at o. Instead, it intersects line BD at no point other than m. Continuing this process for the following points on the trajectory, it turns out that B, like G, must continue its trajectory along the imaginary line. The explanation of why the spiral line of the foot must be somewhat different from that of the center of gravity, and that this difference is quite different for the skater than for the disc, would take me beyond the limits of this essay.

All the planets will fall out of their ellipses into spirals and thus finally fall into the sun as soon as they encounter friction in their orbits.

Even if it were not improper for this setting, it would be superfluous to identify the best kinds of skates at the end.[45] Instead, it is appropriate to add here that, with good skates that are thought to be suitable for edge-running, the sharp part of the blade—I mean the entire lower edge—does not have to be in a straight line such that if you hold both of them together, the edges come together everywhere. More importantly, the blades must have a shallow curvature, so when held together, they touch at only one small spot.[46] The reason for this is too easy to see to require further discussion.*[47]

---

*For edge-running, blades that have a channel filed along their length could have an advantage. If a screw goes from the heel of the blade into the heel of the shoe or boot, the skate acquires great strength and is of particular use to the edge-runner. *[Note added in the 1790 republication.]*

Klopstock's poems

It will not be displeasing to the reader to find three of Klopstock's finest odes, which the author of this treatise refers to, here together. It was thought better not to break up the text or interrupt it with overly long notes, and to share these excellent poems with the enthusiast in this appendix.[48]

Skating

SUNK in the tomb of endless night
    Lies many a great inventor's name:
Our torch we kindle at their light;
    But where is their reward of fame?

How mane ye him, who ocean cross'd   5
    First with tall mast and swelling sheet?
I would not e'en his name were lost
    Who added wings to flying feet.

For should he not immortal live,
    Whose art can health and joy enhance,   10
Such as no mettled steed can give,
    Such, e'en, as pants not in the dance?

Undying still be thy renown!
    The ice-dance, with the gliding steel,
I trace, inventive; flying down   15
    The course, then turn with finer heel.

Thou knowest each inspiring tone
    Of Music. Lend it to the dance!
Her horn resound to wood and moon,
    When rapidly she bids advance!

O youth, whose skill the ice-cothurn
    Drives glowing now, and now restrains,
On city hearths let fagots burn,
    But come with me to crystal plains!

The scene is fill'd with vapoury light,
    As when the winter morning's prime
Looks on the lake. Above it Night
    Scatters, like stars, the glittering rime.

How still and white is all around!
    How rings the track with new-sparr'd frost!
Far off the metal's cymbal-sound
    Betrays thee, for a moment lost.

The wallet bears enough, I ween,
    Of cates and gladsome wine in store?
The winter air makes hunger keen,
    And the foot's flying pinions more.

Turn to the left! I will incline
    My course, half circling, to the right.
Lean forward! take thy stroke from mine!
    So—now shoot by me, like the light!

In undulation serpentine
    Along the shore we downward wend.
Poise not they attitudes too fine!
    Such turns I love not, nor commend.

On Skating

Why to the Isle dost list aloof?
    Unpractised skaters clamour there.
The ice not yet will load and hoof
    Above, nor nets beneath it, bear.

Ah! nought upon thine ear is lost.
    What wailing doth the death-crash make!
How different sounds it, when the frost
    Runs, splitting, miles along the lake!

Turn back! nor let the glacial gleam
    Entice thee onward far from shore!
For there perchance deep waters stream,
    And there the bubbling fountains pour.

By waves unheard above the reef,
    By hidden springs, Death watches nigh.
Though thou glide lightly as the leaf,
    There would'st though sink, young man, and die!

Braga

By Wandor, Wittekind's Bard

> DOST waste in woodlands with the herd thy time,
> And musing slumberest? nor arouseth thee,
> O Tenderling, December's silver rime,
> > Nor star-lights on the crystal see?
>
> I mock to see thee crouch'd in the wolf's hide
> Before the fire, yet bloody from the wound,
> Where the keen arrow pierced the conqueror's side,
> > When he sank helpless to the ground.
>
> Up, then, awake! December never cross'd
> The woodlands with so bright, so soft a ray;
> Nor hoar-white blossoms after nightly frost
> > Flower'd so fair at dawn of day.
>
> Already with the glow of health elate
> Descending swift the frozen shore along,
> The crystal I have whiten'd with my skate
> > In mazes, as to Braga's song.
>
> Beneath the volant foot and metal keen,
> Light borne along the ice, fleet echoes rise.
> Over the mosses by the margin green
> > My flying shadow with me flies.
>
> But now the cloudless moon ascends the sky.
> Her inspiration all my soul pervades
> As drunk at Mimer's fountain! I descry,
> > Far off beneath the bardic shades,

Braga, whose shoulder with no quiver rings,
But 'neath his foot, like silver, sounds the steel.
From night into the moonbeam forth he springs,
    And skims the crystal with light heel.

Sing how the oak-leaves bound his brow sublime
Sing, Bardic song, how, as with pearly dew,
The wreath of Glasor glitter'd with the rime:
    His golden locks were rimy too.

Fiery he woke the strings, and taught the rock
The Telyn's minstrelsy. The brave his lays
Rewarded, and the wise: the strophe's stroke
    Rung joyous forth Walhalla's praise.

"Ha! how my lance is bloody, and calls down
The eagle from the cloud." Along the dance,
Thus singing, like the storm he hastened on,
    Or slacken'd now to slow advance.

"Strike your strong pinions, eagles, for the prey!
Come! drink warm blood! Through the
              dim-glittering air
He scour'd along the course. The God of day,
    Apollo, never sped so fair.

Then lighter turns, disportive, him beseem'd,
And lighter Telyn-tones. "Hear, grove, my strain!
Not by the Hebrus, as the Grecian deem'd,
    Upon the crystal water-plain,

> These wings of steel that can the storm o'ertake,
> Did Thracian Orpheus find, nor down the flood
> Sped to Eurydice; but I, who wake
> > To heroes in the sacred wood
>
> My songs, and Bard and Scald with fire inform,
> I—sound it, Telyn, to the Hebrus!—I
> Invented these, the wingèd shaft and storm,
> > In race victorious to outvie.
>
> The art I taught to Siphia's beauteous son,*
> Around whose foot and arrow lightnings played.
> I taught it Tialf, whom in contest none
> > Outstripped, as erst the Sorcerer's shade.
>
> I taught the bravest of the northern kings;
> Yet him did Russia's proud Eliza shun.
> Would Nossa,† whom the harp immortal sings,
> > Would she have fled him, foolish one?"

He sped. His frosty garland crisp'd aloud,
Back flew his golden hair. The steelly clang
Mellow'd in distance; till in misty cloud
> His form was lost were heights o'erhang.

---

*Siphia's son—Uller. Tialf—Thor's attendant, who held a race with an illusive Giant, raised by sorcery. See Prose Edda. *[Note in the 1790 republication.]*

†The goddess of grace and beauty. *[Note in the 1790 republication.]*

Tialf's Art

By Wittekind's* bards, Bliid, Hainig, and Wandor.

BLIID.

How rings the ice! Stay thy impetuous feet!
    The night-breath glimmers o'er the frozen seas!
Still on thou speedest! From a course too fleet
    Affrighted NOSSA flees.

HAINING.

She follows after. I in rhythmic dance
    O'ertake the shaft fresh-wingèd from the bow.
How the smooth plain resounds to my advance!
    Is NOSSA's foot too slow?

BLIID.

Provoke her not, o'ertaker of the reed!
    Scorn'd she returns no more. I see it now,
Her anger is begun: hold in thy speed!
    The cloud is on her brow.

HAINING.

Dost see them by the rock come down the lake
    In the clear air of bright December morn?
How they wave onward! Dearly will I take
    Revenge of Hlyda's scorn.

---

*WITTEKIND, an able chief of the Saxons who defended them against the invasions of Charlemagne. NOSSA is the goddess of grace. *[Note in the 1790 republication.]*

Bliid.

Who comes? who is it? How they shed a ray
    Of brightness on December's morn so fair!
Ha! thou defamer of the goddess, say
    Who wave through the white air?

Like huntsman's echo from the valley's sides
    The crystal rings melodious to the steel:
And many swing about the chair that glides
    As on self-moving keel.

And who is she, with ermeline beclad,
    Who back-reclining on her chair so light
Lists to the youth behind her, who would add
    Wings to the steel-borne flight?

Haining.

'Twas for the maiden's sake I did defame
    Fair Nossa; nor to pardon is she loth.
The youth and maiden own their mutual flame,
    To-day they seal their troth.

O thou, beclad in ermeline, and thou,
    Whose flying hair is bright with silver rime,
Our bardic dance shall celebrate with you
    The festival sublime.

Wandor.

Be welcome, brothers! Well ye ply your feet
    Along the shore with whistling rushes crown'd.
Yet one condition:—Make we no retreat
    Until the moon goes down!

Far is it to the dance in the hall
    With the descending moon begins to reel.
Ye must hold strong. She who observes us all
    Loves well the flying steel.

Lo! there the skater with the sparkling bowl,   45
    Which the vine-dresser of the Rhine did store
With grape-juice to the brim! It trembles full:
    Let not a drop run o'er!

So round about! and let the horn-notes ring
    To ancient measures of the bridal strain.   50
And then let Braga's flying dances swing
    Upon the starry plain!

HAINING.

He sang. The white-robed Hlyda glided by,
    And horns resounded after. From the sedge
Of either shore her swift companions fly,   55
    Pois'd light on the steel's edge.

"How glassy is the frost! Ah! yonder clang
    Upon the rock, not here! and let thy might
Fall on the wood, destructive axe!" we sang,
    And leant us to the right.   60

"O crystal, ere thou by the sledger's spike,
    Or sharpen'd hoof, or traveller's goad, be cleft,
Numb'd be the hand that did the anvil strike!"
    We sang, and wended left.

⁶⁵ We sang full many a song of skating-time:
    Of the warm west, that all, alas! destroys,
When fades the blossom of the nightly rime:—
    Of hotspring that decoys

The youth, unseen, to death. He plunged forlorn,
    Tinged with his blood the stream, then sank,
⁷⁰   and died!
Of brawny goatherd that on steel-wings borne
    Hastes to o'ertake his bride,

Now by the hundred-colour'd portal-pass
    Rear'd on the Gacier, a triumphal bow
⁷⁵ To conquering Winter! now by meadow grass
    Where the lamb feeds below.—

Of flakes that mar the mirror of the ice,
    They fright the traveller on the crystal plain,
As when in verdant vales the hind descries
⁸⁰   The thunder-drops of rain.

We sang the Northman's snow-skate, with the hide
    Of sea-dog clad. He stoops and shoots below
With lightning speed: then up the snow-hill side
    Mounts toilsomely and slow.

⁸⁵ The prey drips bloody, from his shoulder hung.
    But the glad dance of Tialf's votaries
He knows not. Them the whirlwind sweeps along,
    The shore behind them flies.

They, fleet as thought, through widening circles
        sway,
    As waves the sea-snake in mid ocean lost.
Then sang we timid Ida's first essay
    Upon the glassy frost.

Small was her foot, and glittering was the steel.
    The straps with hoar-frost leaflets she inwove,
And flying-fish, red-spotted. Then we peal
    Our echoes to the grove:

Then to the ruins of the ancient tower;
    And skim the stream as on the boreal blast,
Or now on the soft west. But, ah the hour!
    The moon is sinking fast!

We sought the measur'd dance in the light hall;
    The crackling hearth with the young firs burnt
        bright.
We feasted proudly, and slept sound withal,
    Making the day our night.

Commentary

Notes

1. Falling on the hands is no longer recommended for beginning skaters because it is a good way to break an arm.

2. "Nature makes [a person] skilled, art easy, and practice powerful." The quote is from Victorinus, a third-century Gallic emperor.

3. The original lecture begins with the exclamation "Meine Herren!" (my gentlemen!), which was omitted in the book.

4. This is probably a reference to Friedrich Gottlieb Klopstock (1724–1803). On page ix of the introduction to his translation of Klopstock's *Odes*, William Nind calls Klopstock "the Pindar of Germany."

5. *Motum peristalticum*, or peristalsis, refers to the sequence of muscle contractions that help food move from the esophagus through the digestive tract.

6. Ovid and Wieland are, respectively, Pūblius Ovidius Nāsō (43 BC – 17/18 AD) and Christoph Martin Wieland (1733 – 1813). Ovid was known for his love poetry; Wieland published a work called *Anti-Ovid* in 1752.

7. Nossa is called Hnoss in Old Norse. In *Gylfaginning*,

part of the *Prose Edda*, Snorri Sturluson reports that "Freyia is highest in rank next to Frigg. She was married to someone called Od. Hnoss is the name of their daughter. She is so beautiful that from her name whatever is beautiful and precious is called *hnossir* [treasures]" (Snorri Sturluson, *Edda*, trans. A. Faulkes [London: Everyman, 1987], 29–30).

8. Vieth uses the word *Wasserkothurn*, which Klopstock coined in his poem "Der Eislauf," according to Grimm and Grimm (*Das deutsche Wörterbuch*, s.v. "Wasserkothurn"). Literally, it means "water shoe"—a *kothurn* was a shoe with a thick sole used by actors in classical tragedies, from the Greek *kothornos*. Wahrig (*Deutsches Wörterbuch*, s.v. "Kothurn") adds that *auf einen Kothurn schreiten* (to stride with one of these shoes) means "to be pathetic." Graevenitz (*Das Ornament des Blicks*, 88) remarks that *Wasserkothurn* "may be a strange word for a skate, but for Klopstock it was above all precise: In the beautiful movements and figures of the skaters, the musical art of spoken language comes to life" (my translation).

9. Jeverland is the area surrounding Jever, a city in the East Friesland district of Lower Saxony in northwestern Germany. It was the closest major city to where Vieth grew up.

10. An excerpt from "Die kunst Tialfs" with "they" changed to "we." The translation given here is Nind's (Klopstock, *Odes*, 248).

11. Vieth has "Hookstiefes," which refers to the Hookseiler Tief, the largest canal in the area where he grew up. It runs out to the lake-like Hookseiler Binnentief and eventually to the North Sea. Vieth was born in Hookseil and probably learned to skate on the local canals.

12. An excerpt from Klopstock's poem "Skating" in Nind's translation (Klopstock, *Odes*, 191).

13. The earliest evidence for skating actually comes from Central Europe, not the north. For a full discussion, see B. A. Thurber, *Skates Made of Bone: A History* (Jefferson, NC: McFarland, 2020).

14. *Gylfaginning* reports that Bragi (as he is called in Old Norse) "is renowned for wisdom and especially for eloquence and command of language. Especially he is knowledgable about poetry, and because of him poetry is called *brag*, and from his name a person is said to be a *brag* (chief) of men or women who has eloquence beyond others, whether it is a woman or a man" (Snorri Sturluson, *Edda*, 25). His connection to skating in Norse mythology, if any, is unclear and may well be a fantasy of Klopstock.

15. An excerpt from "Braga" in Nind's translation (Klopstock, *Odes*, 204–205).

16. Ull, Thialfi (or Tialf, as Vieth and Klopstock call him), and several Haralds are mentioned in *Skáldska-*

parmál, the part of the *Prose Edda* dealing with the art of poetry. The Harald Vieth refers to is probably Harald Hardradi, who ruled Norway from 1046 to 1066 and allegedly wrote some verses Vieth quotes later.

17. The connection between Thialfi (Tialf in Vieth and Klopstock) and skating is based on a mistranslation of a passage in *Gylfaginning*. See Thurber, *Skates Made of Bone*, 40–41, for details of the translation and Thurber, "The Myth of Skating History: Building Elitism into a Sport" for a broader discussion.

18. The translation given is Bishop Percy's version of a poem attributed to Harald Hardrada in *Morkinskinna* (Clunies Ross, *The Old Norse Poetic Translations of Thomas Percy*, 194). It is not correct, but neither is Vieth's German translation. They actually match reasonably well. A better translation is "I know how to forge Yggr's (Óðinn) wine (skaldic poetry); I am a swift horseman; on occasion I have practiced swimming. I can slide on skis; I shoot and row well enough; I have command of both harp playing and poetry" (Andersson and Gade, *Morkinskinna*, 149). Note the big difference in the first claim and the confusion between skis and skates.

19. Vieth uses the German terms *Bogenläufer* (edge runner) and *Schieber* (shover) but gives the Dutch equivalents *buten-beens-looper* (literally outside-edge-runner) and *Schuver*.

20. Measurement units were inconsistent at the time of

Vieth's writing, but an eighteenth-century German mile was not equal to today's mile; it was about 9 km or 5.6 of today's standard miles, making a two-mile trip much more impressive than it sounds at first.

21. The "crystal plane" seems to be homage to Klopstock, who refers to ice as crystalline in his skating poems.

22. This skating professor may be someone Vieth met during the years he spent studying at the University of Göttingen. Identifying this person—possibly the first professional skating coach—was would be a nice contribution to skating history. Even Buttingha Wichers (*Schaatsenrijden*, 159) didn't know who this was.

23. *Praenumerando* means "in advance."

24. I've translated the German word *Boxprofessor* literally as "boxing professor." Prize fighting was very popular in Britain during the latter part of the eighteenth century. See Downing ("The Gentleman Boxer") for a discussion of how boxing allowed men to be both "polite and manly." Eighteenth-century manuals of the sport include Mendoza's (*The Modern Art of Boxing*); Mendoza also ran a boxing school (Downing, "The Gentleman Boxer," 340).

25. Vieth recommends turning the skating foot out and beginning to push before putting the free foot down to become the new skating foot.

26. The Vestris family of ballet dancers was well-known in the eighteenth century.

27. An *entrechat* is a ballet jump with the legs crossing quickly or the heels clicking together. Noverre discusses it in *Letters on Dancing and Ballets*, 123–125, noting that "[i]t is generally believed that the legs beat the *temps* of the *entrechat* as the body comes to the ground. ... actually the *entrechat* is executed when it has attained its highest point of elevation. ... Every dancer who executes an *entrechat* knows how long he will take to beat it."

28. Jean-Georges Noverre (1727–1810) was a ballet master known for his *Lettres sur la danse et sur les ballets* (1760), which Vieth quotes later.

29. Bardic dance is a type of social dance that Vieth lists alongside English country dances and waltzes in his encyclopedia, which includes chapters on both skating and dance. He notes that "sustained and slurred notes" are suited to this dance style (Vieth, *Versuch einer Encyklopädie der Leibesübungen*, II.355).

30. Vieth quotes Noverre's French here, putting together several different parts of the letter. I have pulled the relevant sentences from Beaumont's English translation of *Letters on Dancing and Ballets* (pages 117, 118, and 126), which is based on the 1803 edition—some 13 years after Vieth's book—with ellipses and brackets added to mark lacunae in Vieth's quotation.

31. *Port de bras* refers to a dancer's arm movements.

32. The names Vieth drops are Ernst Platner, German anthropologist, 1744–1818; Edmund Burke, Irish philospher and economist, 1729–1797; and William Hogarth, English artist and satirist, 1697–1764.

33. This is a paraphrase from Klopstock's poem "Die kunst Tialfs." The original poem says *Die Lauscherin hier / liebt flüchtigen Stahl*, which Nind translates as "She who observes us all / Loves well the flying steel" (Klopstock, *Odes*, 245).

34. Modern editions of the poem call this character *Bliid*, but Vieth calls him *Wliid* in both versions of the text. The earlier version of Vieth's text, published in *Neue Litteratur und Völkerkunde*, was written in fraktur, the old German black-letter script, where B (𝕭) and W (𝖂) look similar. Vieth's use of *Wliid* may represent confusion between the two letters. If so, the confusion goes way back: I found *Wliid* in the 1776 edition of Klopstock's *Odes* published in Karlsruhe in fraktur (pp. 257–265), and *Bliid* in the first volume of Klopstock's collected works (*Werke*) published in Leipzig in 1798 (pp. 260–265) in roman type. Nind's translation, quoted here, uses *Bliid*, which I have kept here and in the complete version given later.

35. The word Vieth uses for "vaulters" is *Voltigeurs*, which became the term a type of military unit in Napoleon's

army in 1804. Since Vieth wrote in the late 1780s, he did not know of these fighters. Vieth's comment on horses presumably refers to trick riding.

36. Vieth's "fundamental laws of motion" are drawn from Newton's *Philosophiæ Naturalis Principia Mathematica (Mathematical Principles of Natural Philosophy)*, first published in 1687.

37. Newton proves this in corollary 1 to his laws of motion. See Dana Densmore, *Newton's Principia: The Central Argument*, 3rd ed (Santa Fe, NM: Green Lion Press, 2010), 32–33, for details.

38. The "horizontal plane" is generally the ground, or, in skating, the ice surface.

39. Try laying a pencil sideways across one finger, so that your finger holds it up at one point. When the pencil stays balanced, your finger is under its center of gravity.

40. Vieth uses the German word *Sekunde*, which means "second," but I have translated it as "instant" because the exact length of time is not important as long as it is short, preferably shorter than a second. Using "instant" also avoids undesirable phrases such as "in the second second."

41. Point C is at the center of the spiral the skater is making.

42. The skating foot is the foot on the ice. Vieth calls it the *streichenden Fuß* (stroking foot).

43. The free foot is the foot that's not on the ice. Vieth calls it the *aufgehobnen Fuß* (lifted foot).

44. Fowler, *On the Outside Edge*, 60, says of this passage,

    At the end Vieth refers to further "artificialities," but dismisses them somewhat contemptuously, citing only the **OF** loop **3**, the earliest mention of a loop **3** in literature.

45. Vieth probably learned to skate on Frisian skates of some type. The Breinermoor skate (figure C1) is a strong candidate: it was produced in the German part of East Frisa—where Vieth grew up—starting in about 1750. Breinermoors are low skates with blades that extend well past the skater's toe in front but end at mid-heel (Frits Locher, "Breinermoor," *Schaatshistorie.nl*, 2018, https://www.schaatshistorie.nl/de-schaats/schaatsmodellen/breinermoor/).

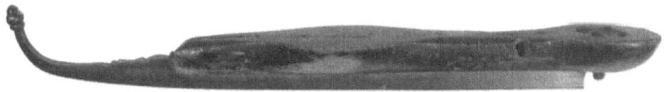

Figure C1: A Breinermoor skate.

46. Vieth is describing rockering of the blades. When you hold two blades together, bottom to bottom, they only touch in one place because they are curved.

47. In the footnote, the editor describes hollow-ground blades and heel screws. Grinding a hollow into a blade gives a definite advantage, but other authors (e.g., Robert Jones, whose *Treatise on Skating* was first published in 1772) caution against it. Attaching the blade firmly to the boot with a screw is a big improvement over the straps that were commonly used in the early days of metal-bladed skates.

48. This text was included as a footnote in the 1790 edition. William Nind's 1848 translations of the poems in question are reproduced here.

Further reading

If you haven't read Robert Jones' *Treatise on Skating*, you should. That's another important source of information on eighteenth-century skating, albeit in England, not Germany.

Fowler* remarks that "Thanks to the energy of the editor of *Deutscher Eis-Sport*, in reprinting in 1895–96 selections from early German works relating to skating, there is a very good record of the history of the art in Germany." This collection appears to be *Der Eis-Sport vor hundert Jahren*, a 58-page volume assembled by O. Schöning that seems only to be available at the British Library.† Of course, it is in German.

There is more available about Vieth's life and his contributions to physical education. Gerhard Lukas wrote a biography of him‡ in German; I have not found one in English. However, Vieth's book on physics for kids§ was translated into English in 1800 and is now available in Google Books.

---

*Fowler, *On the Outside Edge*, 60.

†O. Schöning, ed., *Der Eis-Sport vor hundert Jahren* (Berlin: Deutscher Eis-Sport, 1896).

‡Gerhard Lukas, *Gerhard Ulrich Anton Vieth: Sein Leben und Werk* (Berlin: Sportverlag, 1964).

§G. U. A. Vieth, *The Pleasing Preceptor: Or Familiar Instructions in Natural History and Physics, Adapted to the Capacities of Youth* (London: C. and J. Robinson, 1801).

Bibliography

Andersson, Theodore M., and Kari Ellen Gade. *Morkinskinna: The Earliest Icelandic Chronicle of the Norwegian Kings (1030–1157)*. Icelandica 51. Ithaca: Cornell University Press, 2000.

Brown, Nigel. *Ice-Skating: A History*. London: Nicholas Kaye Limited, 1959.

Clunies Ross, Margaret. *The Old Norse Poetic Translations of Thomas Percy*. Making the Middle Ages 4. Turnhout, Belgium: Brepols, 2001.

Densmore, Dana. *Newton's Principia: The Central Argument*. 3rd ed. Santa Fe, NM: Green Lion Press, 2010.

Downing, Karen. "The Gentleman Boxer: Boxing, Manners, and Masculinity in Eighteenth-Century England." *Men and Masculinities* 12, no. 3 (2010): 328–352. https://doi.org/10.1177/1097184X08318181.

Euler, C. "Vieth, Gerhard Ulrich Anton." *Allgemeine Deutsche Biographie* 38 (1895): 682–684. https://www.deutsche-biographie.de/sfz83762.html.

Fowler, G. Herbert. *On the Outside Edge: Being Diversions in the History of Skating*. Edited by B. A. Thurber. Evanston, IL: Skating History Press, 2018.

Graevenitz, Gerhart von. *Das Ornament des Blicks: Über die Grundlagen des neuzeitlichen Sehens, die Poetik der Arabeske und Goethes "West-östlichen Divan".* Stuttgart: Verlag J. B. Metzler, 1994.

Grimm, Jacob, and Wilhelm Grimm. *Das deutsche Wörterbuch.* Online. Trier, 1998–2004.

GutsMuths, Johann Christoph Friedrich. *Gymnastik für die Jugend: Enthaltend eine praktische Anweisung zu Leibesübungen.* Schnepfenthal: Buchhandlung der Erziehungsanstalt, 1793.

Helfrich, George. "Henriette Sontag." Translated by Mrs. William Amory. *Skating*, May 1926, 39–41.

Hines, James R. *End of the Compulsories: A Remembrance.* n.p.: Self-published, 2022.

Jahn, Friedrich Ludwig, and Ernst Eiselen. *Die deutsche Turnkunst zur Einrichtung der Turnplätze.* Berlin: Self-published, 1816.

Jones, R., and W. E. Cormack. *A Treatise on Skating.* Edited by B. A. Thurber. Evanston, IL: Skating History Press, 2017.

Klopstock, Friedrich Gottlieb. *Klopstocks Werke, Band 1: Oden, Band 1.* Leipzig: Georg Joachim Göschen, 1798.

———. *Oden von Klopstock.* Karlsruhe: Christian Gottlieb Schmieder, 1776.

———. *Odes of Klopstock from 1747 to 1780.* Translated by William Nind. London: William Pickering, 1848.

Locher, Frits. "Breinermoor." *Schaatshistorie.nl*, 2018. https://www.schaatshistorie.nl/de-schaats/schaatsmodellen/breinermoor/.

Lukas, Gerhard. *Gerhard Ulrich Anton Vieth: Sein Leben und Werk.* Berlin: Sportverlag, 1964.

Meissner, R. "Zum Hildebrandslied." *Zeitschrift für deutsches Altertum und deutsche Literatur* N. F. 30 (= 42) (1898): 122–128.

Mendoza, Daniel. *The Modern Art of Boxing.* London: n.p., 1789.

Noverre, Jean Georges. *Letters on Dancing and Ballets.* Translated by Cyril W. Beaumont. London: C. W. Beaumont, 1930.

Schöning, O., ed. *Der Eis-Sport vor hundert Jahren.* Berlin: Deutscher Eis-Sport, 1896.

"Hines." *Skating* 99, no. 10 (December 2022): 47.

Snorri Sturluson. *Edda.* Translated by A. Faulkes. London: Everyman, 1987.

Thurber, B. A. *Skates Made of Bone: A History.* Jefferson, NC: McFarland, 2020.

———. "The Myth of Skating History: Building Elitism into a Sport." *Leisure Sciences* 43, no. 6 (2021): 562–574.

Trunz, Erich, ed. *Goethes Werke: Hamburger Ausgabe in 14 Bänden*. Vol. 9. Hamburg: C. Wegner, 1948.

Vieth, G. U. A. "Der Eislauf." In *Das gesammte Turnwesen: Ein Lesebuch für deutsche Turner*, edited by Georg Hirth, 216–230. Leipzig: Ernst Keil, 1865.

———. *The Pleasing Preceptor: Or Familiar Instructions in Natural History and Physics, Adapted to the Capacities of Youth*. London: C. and J. Robinson, 1801.

———. "Ueber das Schrittschuhlaufen." *Neue Litteratur und Völkerkunde*, 1789, 100–126.

———. *Versuch einer Encyklopädie der Leibesübungen*. Berlin: Carl Ludwig Hartmann, 1795.

Vieth, Gerhard Ulrich Anton. *Ueber das Schrittschuhlaufen*. Leipzig: Graz Widmanstätter, 1790.

Wahrig, Gerhard. *Deutsches Wörterbuch*. Gütersloh: Bertelsmann Lexikon-Verlag, 1975.

Zindel, Christian Siegmund. *Der Eislauf*. Nürnberg: Friedrich Campe, 1825.

Illustration credits

Cover Background: "Old Paper Floral Parchment Background" from *MyFreeTextures* (www.myfreetextures.com).

Author portrait: "Gerhard Ulrich Anton Vieth" from G. U. A. Vieth, "Der Eislauf," in *Das gesammte Turnwesen: Ein Lesebuch für deutsche Turner*, ed. Georg Hirth (Leipzig: Ernst Keil, 1865), 216–230. Digitized by Google Books and cropped by B. A. Thurber.

Skater drawing: "Fig. 1" from G. U. A. Vieth, "Ueber das Schrittschuhlaufen," *Neue Litteratur und Völkerkunde*, 1789, 100–126, with modifications by B. A. Thurber. Original digitized by Google Books.

1 Author portrait from Vieth's chapter on skating in the copy of *Das gesammte Turnwesen* in the Bayern State Library, between pages 216 and 217. Digitized by Google Books and modified by B. A. Thurber.

2 Image by Happolati, courtesy of Wikimedia Commons. Used under a CC-by-sa 3.0 license.

3 Image by M_H.DE, courtesy of Wikimedia Commons. Used under a CC-by-sa 3.0 license.

p. 30 Unnumbered image sketched on the endpaper of the copy of Gerhard Ulrich Anton Vieth, *Ueber das Schrittschuhlaufen* (Leipzig: Graz Widmanstätter, 1790) at the Czech National Library. Digitized by Google Books and modified by B. A. Thurber.

4–7 Images from the copy of Vieth's article, G. U. A. Vieth, "Ueber das Schrittschuhlaufen," *Neue Litteratur und Völkerkunde*, 1789, 100–126, in the Czech National Library, between pages 126 and 127. Digitized by Google Books

C1 Image courtesy of Frits Locher, also available on *Schaatshistorie.nl*, s.v. "Breinermoor."

www.ingramcontent.com/pod-product-compliance
Lightning Source LLC
Chambersburg PA
CBHW030158100526
44592CB00009B/346